CLASSIC TARTS

for every occasion

CLASSIC TARTS

for every occasion

RYLAND
PETERS
& SMALL

Maxine Clark

photography by Martin Brigdale

First published in Great Britain in 2003
This edition 2005

by Ryland Peters & Small
20–21 Jockey's Fields
London WC1R 4BW
www.rylandpeters.com

10 9 8 7 6 5 4 3 2 1

Printed in China

ISBN 1 84597 058 6

A CIP record for this book is available
from the British Library.

Designers Saskia Janssen, Steve Painter,
        Megan Smith
Commissioning Editor Elsa Petersen-Schepelern
Editors Kim Davis, Elsa Petersen-Schepelern
Production Sheila Smith
Art Director Gabriella Le Grazie
Publishing Director Alison Starling

Food Stylists Maxine Clark, Linda Tubby
Prop Stylist Helen Trent
Indexer Hilary Bird

Notes

- All spoon measurements are level unless otherwise specified.
- All eggs are medium, unless otherwise specified. Uncooked or partly cooked eggs should not be served to the very young, the very old, those with compromised immune systems, or pregnant women.
- Before baking, weigh or measure all ingredients exactly and prepare baking tins or sheets.
- Ovens should be preheated to the specified temperature. Recipes in this book were tested in several kinds of oven – all work slightly differently. I recommend using an oven thermometer. Most fan-assisted ovens, for instance, are set 20 degrees lower than regular ovens. Consult the maker's handbook. This is important when baking.
- All microwaves differ in power output, so be guided by the maker's handbook. The times given here are only guidelines – you must get to know your own microwave.

Author's Dedication

Dedicated to my sister Jacks, my friend, who is known to make a decent tart or two, and is a constant source of inspiration.

Author's acknowledgements

Thanks to all those listed below for helping to create this beautiful book.

Elsa, for asking me to do this book and being a kindly dragon where necessary.

Kim, for her good-humoured and efficient editing.

Steve for his elegant design and calm control during photography – and his great taste in tarts.

Martin for his luscious, light, atmospheric photography and his relish for a good tart.

Helen for her simply spectacular styling and boundless enthusiasm.

And Becca Hetherston, without whose good-humoured assistance in all things tarty at the studio, I could not have managed.

contents

a treat for tart lovers

I just love making tarts, and have done so ever since watching my grandmother baking tartlets for us when we came home from school, and letting us fill them with lemon curd. But then it's in the genes, you see: I come from a family of bakers and I am Scottish (we love to bake).

Making your own pastry well is one of the simple pleasures in life. Your own pastry bears no resemblance to the bought stuff in either taste or texture, AND you can monitor the ingredients. Ready-to-roll pastry made with real butter is almost impossible to find in Britain, and I will not accept hydrogenated vegetable fat as an ingredient for pastry. It produces pastry with no flavour and a colourless appearance. Whatever fat you use, it must be pure, and your flour good quality. Good ingredients make great dishes.

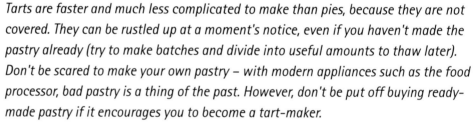

Tarts are faster and much less complicated to make than pies, because they are not covered. They can be rustled up at a moment's notice, even if you haven't made the pastry already (try to make batches and divide into useful amounts to thaw later). Don't be scared to make your own pastry – with modern appliances such as the food processor, bad pastry is a thing of the past. However, don't be put off buying ready-made pastry if it encourages you to become a tart-maker.

The majority of tarts in this book are sweet – it naturally worked out that way – but there are recipes for everyday tarts, tarts for a special occasion, classic tarts and comfortingly self-indulgent tarts. People notice when they bite into a homemade crust, revealing a heavenly interior, so get to grips with pastry-making and you'll never look back. Like baking your own bread, it is a very satisfying and rewarding experience. Go ahead and tackle a tart today!

equipment and utensils

A large work surface or marble slab is essential. Never roll out pastry in a cramped area (you may roll unevenly or stretch the pastry). The surface should be cool (not next to the stove) to stop the pastry turning soft and unmanageable.

Accurate weighing scales to get the quantities and proportions correct.

Measuring spoons are necessary for all baking. Recipes in this book require all measurements to be level.

Heatproof measuring jugs, large and small, are dual purpose; use to measure liquid ingredients, and also in the microwave (which I use as a kitchen tool like all other equipment).

Fine and medium sieves sift flour to aerate it and remove lumps, making for a lighter pastry. Icing sugar should ALWAYS be sifted in a fine sieve – the lumps will never beat out.

Assorted mixing bowls – plastic, stainless steel, glass or Pyrex are all suitable. Make sure they are big enough; you need plenty of room to move for your hands and the ingredients when rubbing in. This, too, aerates the pastry.

A food processor is a MUST if you have hot hands, or if you think you can't make pastry. It removes all the fear of butter melting into the flour, because it mixes fat and flour so quickly and evenly. Always pulse the machine when adding liquids so that the dough will not be overworked and become tough.

A flour sifter/shaker, though not absolutely necessary, does stop you adding too much flour to the work surface or pastry. Too much extra flour destroys the proportions and affects taste and texture.

Several pastry brushes so you always have a dry one to hand for brushing excess flour off pastry, and one for brushing liquids and glazes.

A pastry scraper to scrape the pastry off a work surface, and for cleaning off all the messy bits. Indispensable.

A palette knife can be used instead, but is best used for chopping in the flour in French pastries such as pâte brisée (page 15).

Microplane graters were a revelation to me, and once acquired, you'll wonder how you ever lived without them. There are three grades – fine, medium and coarse. Fine is for grating lemons, nutmeg, garlic, ginger and Parmesan cheese; medium for other cheeses, and general grating; and coarse is for grating butter into pastry or grating streusel-type pastry.

A pastry blender is something I have used only occasionally, but some cooks swear by it. It is a series of thin metal loops connected to a handle, which you use to cut the fat into the flour. It prevents 'hot hand syndrome' and aerates the pastry. I prefer an old round-bladed cutlery knife (or two – one in each hand) to cut in the fat.

All-purpose clingfilm or plastic bags are absolutely necessary to wrap pastry before chilling or freezing, protecting it and preventing it from drying out.

A bottle of iced water – always keep one in the refrigerator so you have chilled water to hand for pastry-making.

CHOOSING TART TINS

Good solid baking sheets that won't buckle in the oven are ESSENTIAL.

Tart tins – choose a selection of sizes, with removable bases. The heavier the tins are the better, so they won't buckle. Heavy tins will cook the tart or pastry more evenly. Traditionally, fluted edges designated sweet fillings while plain edges indicated a savoury filling. The most useful sizes are 20.5, 23, 25 cm and sometimes a 30 cm for a crowd.

Some people prefer flan rings to set on a baking sheet, instead of loose-based tins. Strong and easy to store, the most useful are 20.5, 23 and 25 cm.

A tarte Tatin pan This is a heavy-based tin specially designed to conduct the heat well to caramelize the apples without burning. Two sizes – 20 and 28 cm.

Metal or enamel pie plates with wide rim to take a good crust. Used for American-style tarts and pies, and tarts that need a decorative edge such as treacle tart. Two sizes – 20.5 and 23 cm, deep or shallow.

Assorted springform tins for deeper tarts. Useful are 20.5, 23 and 25 cm.

Tartlet tins in various sizes and shapes. I collect these and find that the most useful are loose-based, 9–10 cm for individual tarts, 6–7 cm for tartlets.

Patty pans/tins are the traditional tins for making little tartlets in bulk, like curd or jam tarts.

Mini muffin tins are wonderful for making cocktail-sized tartlets in bulk and little filo tartlets.

Yorkshire pudding tins (4-hole) make larger individual shallow tarts in bulk, and fit into the oven nicely.

ROLLING OUT AND LINING THE TIN

A ruler to check tin sizes and cutting straight edges when decorating pastry.

A long straight rolling pin (wooden or nylon) with no handles – handles spoil the even rolling action of the pin. Always keep pins where the surface won't be damaged by other kitchen utensils (not in the utensil drawer). If using a rolling pin to smash or pound, use the end, not the long surface, or it will become pitted and transfer marks onto the pastry.

A sharp cook's knife or thin-bladed filleting knife for trimming – razor-sharp to cut the pastry and not drag it.

A large serrated knife for trimming and slicing – this stays nice and sharp and is good for cutting baked pastry shells.

A fork for pricking bases and decorating.

Palette knives – I have 3 sizes: large to help loosen rolled-out pastry from the work surface; small to lift little pastry circles into a tart tin; and a tiny one to lift pastry decorations onto the tart edge.

Clingfilm, greaseproof paper, kitchen foil, non-stick baking parchment for wrapping pastry, lining tart tins and baking blind.

Baking beans (ceramic or metal) or a jar of rice or dried beans which can be used over and over for baking blind.

Biscuit cutters, both plain and fluted, to cut out small tarts to line tartlet tins, bun tins or mini muffin tins.

DECORATING PASTRY

Biscuit cutters can be used to create dozens of decorative edges using leaf cutters, shaped cutters (even animals) to customize your tarts.

Pastry wheels to cut straight lines and give decorative edges.

A small sharp knife will help to cut patterns on decorations.

A lattice cutter is a clever way of making a professional-looking lattice top for tarts and pies.

BAKING AND COOLING TARTS

Electronic timer – I think that it's impossible to cook pastry and not burn it without one.

Oven gloves – a must, no damp tea towels to burn your hands.

Wire or metal cooling racks – assorted sizes, 1 large and 2 medium.

Mesh cloches or domes are useful for protecting the tart against damage as it cools, letting the air circulate freely.

A large slice or cake-lifter to help lift the tart onto a plate without it falling to bits.

A serrated palette knife is useful for slicing the tart, then serving or lifting onto a plate.

top tart tips

• Water/liquid quantities are never exact as there are so many variables. Add slightly less than is stated, because you can always add more – but too much and the pastry is lost.

• Always have a dry pastry brush on hand to remove excess flour.

• If your hands are sticky with dough, stop everything and wash them, then dry them and dust with flour. This will stop the pastry sticking to them and prevent horrible dry flaky bits falling off your hands into the pastry when you roll it out.

• Try to flour your hands and the rolling pin rather than bathing the pastry in flour to prevent sticking.

• When rolling pastry, keep it moving on a 'Hovercraft' of flour and it will never stick.

• Roll pastry directly on a piece of non-stick baking parchment or clingfilm so it can be moved around easily without sticking to the work surface.

• Roll directly away from you and move the pastry around by short turns in one direction so you roll it evenly.

• Setting two chopsticks (or similar) on either side of a piece of dough before you roll it out will help you to roll it evenly to the thickness of the chopstick and no less.

• If you are a beginner, don't try to roll out the pastry too thin – just cook for a bit longer when you bake blind (page 22).

• There is no need to grease a tin before lining. All pastry has fat in it and is effectively non-stick – it is the filling leaking out over the edges or through holes that makes pastry stick.

• When you line a tart tin, try rolling the flour-dusted pastry around the rolling pin to help you to pick it up – this will avoid stretching the pastry and stop it shrinking when cooking.

• Use a small piece of pastry wrapped in clingfilm to help to push the pastry into the edges of the tin. Once this is done, you can press the pastry up the sides of the tin and cut off the overhang with a very sharp knife. I like to press the pastry into the flutes of the ring after cutting off the excess to give a good shape.

• If in doubt, CHILL, CHILL, CHILL! Raw pastry will benefit from thorough chilling at every stage. I like to freeze pastry-lined tins before baking blind as this really sets the pastry, so it holds its shape. Freeze the unbaked tart shell after lining the tin with pastry, even just for 15 minutes. It rests the pastry and makes the tart easy to line with foil and beans when baking blind. Work quickly and get it into the oven before it thaws, then you will have a perfect tart shell.

• Always chill a double crust pie before baking.

• Always glaze, then chill a pie before making any marks on the pastry – it will be easier to do.

• Always chill a pie before making slits in the pastry.

• Always place a tart on a baking sheet before baking. This will make it easier to lift in and out of the oven and prevent any spillage burning on the bottom of the oven.

• If travelling with the tart, put it back in the ring to make carrying easier and safer, and wrap in a clean tea towel.

• Care of equipment – metal tins should be washed gently in warm, soapy water, then rinsed and dried thoroughly (in the turned-off oven after baking), or they will rust. Some tins should just be wiped with kitchen paper – this will gradually build up a non-stick patina on the surface.

Pastry can be made by hand, or in a food processor. If you have cool hands, the hand method is best because more air will be incorporated. If you have hot hands, the food processor is a blessing. The quantities of water added vary according to the humidity of the flour, so always add less than the recipe says – you can add more if the dough is dry.

basic shortcrust pastry

250 g plain flour

a pinch of salt

50 g lard (or white cooking fat), chilled and diced

75 g unsalted butter, chilled and diced

2–3 tablespoons chilled water

makes about 400 g pastry, enough to line a tart tin 23–25 cm diameter or to make a double crust for a deep pie plate 20–23 cm diameter

Sift the flour and salt together into a bowl. Alternatively, sift into a food processor.

Rub in the lard and butter until the mixture resembles breadcrumbs. If using a food processor, blend for 30 seconds for the same result.

Add the water, mixing lightly with a knife to bring the pastry together. If using a food processor, pulse for 10 seconds until the pastry forms large lumps. If necessary, add another tablespoon of water and pulse again.

Knead lightly on a floured work surface, then shape into a flattened ball, wrap in clingfilm and chill for at least 30 minutes before rolling out.

Note The quantities given here are generous. Leftover pastry may be frozen.

rich shortcrust pastry

250 g plain flour

1/2 teaspoon salt

125 g unsalted butter, chilled and diced

2 medium egg yolks

2 tablespoons iced water

makes about 400 g pastry, enough to line a tart tin 23–25 cm diameter or to make a double crust for a deep pie plate 20–23 cm diameter

Sift the flour and salt together into a bowl, then rub in the butter. Mix the egg yolks with the 2 tablespoons iced water. Add to the flour, mixing together lightly with a knife. The dough must have some water in it or it will be too difficult to handle. If it is still too dry, add a little more water, sprinkling it over the flour mixture 1 tablespoon at a time.

Transfer the mixture to a lightly floured work surface. Knead lightly with your hands until smooth. Form the dough into a rough ball. Flatten slightly, then wrap in plastic wrap and chill for at least 30 minutes before rolling out.

Sweet Rich Shortcrust Pastry Sift 2 tablespoons icing sugar with the flour and salt.

making pastry

This is a recipe for the classic American pie crust, given to me by a good friend from New York State. The quantity is enough for two tarts; she makes and bakes one straight away and freezes the rest for another time. You could make and bake both tarts now, freeze all the dough to use later, or make a double quantity and freeze it all. To give the crust a richer flavour and delightful golden colour, unsalted butter can be substituted for the cooking fat, or you can use half butter and half cooking fat (or lard). It has a very light, crumbly pastry when baked – similar to shortcrust and very homely.

american pie crust

375 g plain flour

a good pinch of salt

250 g white cooking fat, chilled

1 medium egg, beaten

1 tablespoon wine vinegar or lemon juice

4 tablespoons iced water

makes about 675 g pastry, enough for 2 deep tart shells 24 cm diameter

Sift the flour and salt into a large bowl. Cut in the fat using 2 round-bladed knives or a pastry blender (or do this in a food processor).

Beat the egg in a separate bowl or jug. Stir in the vinegar, then add the water.

Pour the wet mixture into the dry mixture, then cut it in with the knives or pastry blender again. Using your hands, quickly bring the dough together. Knead until smooth either in the bowl or on a floured work surface. Cut in half so it's easier to roll out later.

Shape the dough into a flattened ball, wrap in clingfilm, then chill for at least 30 minutes before rolling out.

To bake, cut in half. Roll out each piece to about 3 mm thick. Line both tart tins, prick all over with a fork and chill or freeze for 15 minutes. Line with foil or all-purpose clingfilm and fill with baking beans. For partial baking, bake at 200°C (400°F) Gas 6 for 10–12 minutes. For full baking, cook for 15–18 minutes until just colouring around the edges. Remove the foil or clingfilm and beans (cool and reserve the beans to use again), then return the tart shells to the oven to dry out for 4–5 minutes until golden.

To freeze, cut the uncooked pastry in half and form each piece into flattened balls ready to thaw and roll out.

dill and nutmeg pastry

250 g plain flour

a pinch of salt

1 teaspoon freshly grated nutmeg

4 tablespoons chopped fresh dill

125 g unsalted butter,
chilled and diced

1 medium egg yolk

2–3 tablespoons iced water

makes about 400 g pastry,
enough to line a tart tin
23–25 cm diameter or to
make a double crust for a deep
pie plate 20–23 cm diameter

Put the flour, salt, nutmeg and dill in a food processor, add the butter and blend until the mixture looks like fine breadcrumbs. Mix the egg yolk with the iced water and add to the machine. Blend again until it begins to form a ball – add another tablespoon of water if it is too dry and blend again. Tip out onto a floured work surface and knead lightly until smooth, then shape into a flattened ball. Wrap in clingfilm and chill for 30 minutes before rolling.

cheese shortcrust pastry

225 g plain flour

1 teaspoon salt

3 tablespoons freshly grated
Parmesan cheese

125 g unsalted butter

2 medium egg yolks

2–3 tablespoons iced water

makes about 400 g pastry,
enough to line a tart tin
23–25 cm diameter or to make
a double crust for a deep pie
plate 20–23 cm diameter

Sift the flour and salt into a bowl. Stir in the Parmesan, then rub in the butter. Mix the egg yolks with 2 tablespoons iced water, then stir into the flour mixture to bind to a firm but malleable dough. If it is too dry, add another tablespoon of water and blend again. Knead lightly until smooth, then shape into a flattened ball. Wrap in clingfilm and chill for at least 30 minutes before rolling out.

This is the classic French sweet pastry sometimes known as pâte sablée or 'sandy pastry', because it has a fine crumbly texture when broken. Its high sugar content means that it can burn very easily – use a timer. It takes slightly longer to blind bake than other pastries – bake at the standard 190°C (375°F) Gas 5 for 15 minutes, then reduce the temperature to 180°C (350°F) Gas 4 and cook for a further 10 minutes to dry out completely.

pâte sucrée

200 g plain flour

a pinch of salt

75 g caster or icing sugar

75 g unsalted butter, diced, at room temperature

2 medium egg yolks

$1/2$ teaspoon real vanilla essence

2–3 tablespoons iced water

makes about 400 g pastry, enough to line a tart tin 25 cm diameter or 6 tartlet tins 9 cm diameter

Classic Method

Sift the flour, salt and sugar into a mound on a clean work surface. Make a well in the middle with your fist.

Put the butter, egg yolks and vanilla essence in the well. Using the fingers of one hand, 'peck' the eggs and butter together until the mixture resembles creamy scrambled eggs.

Flick the flour over the egg mixture and chop it through with a palette knife or pastry scraper, until it is almost amalgamated but looking very lumpy. Sprinkle with the water and chop again.

Bring together quickly with your hands. Knead lightly into a ball, then flatten slightly. Wrap in clingfilm, then chill for at least 30 minutes before using. Let it return to room temperature before rolling out.

Food Processor Method

Put the sugar, butter, egg yolks and vanilla essence in a food processor, then blend until smooth. Add the water and blend again.

Sift the flour and salt onto a sheet of greaseproof paper, then add to the processor. Blend until just combined. Transfer the dough to a lightly floured work surface. Knead gently until smooth. Form into a flattened ball, then wrap in clingfilm. Chill or freeze for at least 30 minutes. Let it return to room temperature before rolling out. This is quite a delicate pastry to roll, so be sure to use enough (but not too much) flour when rolling.

The French version of an unsweetened shortcrust, pâte brisée has a finer texture, so should be rolled out much thinner – to about 3 mm. Sometimes pâte brisée is used for fruit tarts that are baked for a long time, because other pastries with high sugar content would scorch before the fruit was cooked. This one gives a firm, crisp support for the fruit. Don't omit the water in either this or the pâte sucrée opposite – it makes the pastry stronger and easier to handle in the end.

pâte brisée

200 g plain flour

a large pinch of salt

100 g unsalted butter, diced, at room temperature

1 medium egg yolk

2¹/₂–3 tablespoons iced water

makes about 350 g pastry, enough to line a tart tin 25 cm diameter or 6 tartlet tins 9 cm diameter

Classic Method

Sift the flour and salt into a mound on a clean work surface. Make a well in the middle with your fist.

Put the butter and egg yolk in the well and using the fingers of one hand 'peck' the eggs and butter together until they resemble scrambled eggs.

Using a palette knife or pastry scraper, flick the flour over the egg mixture and chop through until almost amalgamated. Sprinkle with the water and chop again.

Bring together quickly with your hands. Knead lightly into a ball, then flatten slightly. Wrap in clingfilm and chill for at least 30 minutes. Let it return to room temperature before rolling out.

Food Processor Method

Sift the flour and salt together onto a sheet of greaseproof paper.

Put the butter and egg yolk in a food processor and blend until smooth, then add the water and blend again. Add the flour and salt and pulse until just mixed.

Transfer to a lightly floured work surface and knead gently until smooth. Form into a ball, flatten slightly and wrap in clingfilm. Chill in the refrigerator for at least 30 minutes. Let the pastry return to room temperature before rolling out.

Note Ovens vary, so you may need slightly lower settings than these for this recipe and the one opposite.

This is the most difficult of all the layered pastries but, once mastered, it is relatively easy to do as long as you stick to the rules of resting and chilling. It is worth the effort – the flavour and texture means it is like biting into a buttery cloud. Classic puff pastry involves dotting the dough with lard and butter before rolling and folding. It is a more complicated version of rough puff, which is the one I prefer. Unless otherwise stated, blind bake puff pastry at 230°C (450°F) Gas 8, to enable it to rise quickly, then lower the temperature to 200°C (400°F) Gas 6 for the final drying-out stage.

classic puff pastry

250 g plain or strong plain flour

¼ teaspoon salt

250 g unsalted butter, in 1 piece,
at cool room temperature
(it must be malleable,
but not melting)

1 teaspoon lemon juice

about 150 ml iced water

makes about 550 g pastry,
enough to line a tart tin
30 cm diameter

Sift the flour and salt into a large bowl. Rub in one-quarter of the butter with the tips of your fingers. Sprinkle with the lemon juice and not quite all the water. Mix with a round-bladed knife until the dough starts to come together in a lump. If the mixture is dry, add the rest of the water, 1 tablespoon at a time.

Tip the pastry onto a floured work surface. Knead lightly to form a smooth ball. Flatten the ball with the palm of your hand, then wrap the pastry in clingfilm and chill for about 30 minutes until firm.

Put the remaining butter between sheets of baking parchment, then roll or beat with a rolling pin to make a square about 1 cm thick. Unwrap the pastry and roll out into a square large enough to wrap around the butter. Put the butter in the centre of the pastry. Bring the edges up and over to cover the butter completely.

Dust the rolling pin and both sides of the pastry parcel with flour. Using the rolling pin, make 3–4 impressions on the surface of the parcel to start the pastry rolling.

Rolling and Folding

Roll into a rectangle about 3 times longer than it is wide – you don't need exact measurements, but the pastry should be about 1 cm thick. Remove excess flour with a dry pastry brush.

Lightly mark the rectangle into 3 equal sections, using the blunt edge of a knife. Fold the third that is closest to you up over the middle third. Bring the top third towards you over the folded two-thirds. (This will be the first roll and fold.)

Give the pastry a quarter-turn anticlockwise so it looks like a closed book, with the long open edge to the right. Make a finger mark in the pastry to remind you that you have rolled and folded it once (next time, make 2 marks). Rewrap and chill for 15 minutes.

Return the pastry to the work surface in the closed-book position. Seal the 3 edges lightly with a rolling pin to stop them sliding out of shape. Roll out, away from you in one direction only, until the pastry forms the same-sized rectangle as before. Fold in the same way as before, wiping off any excess flour with the pastry brush. (It is important to be consistent about the direction of rolling and folding in order to build up the leaves of the pastry; always start with the long open edge to your right.)

Make 2 indentations in the the pastry (indicating 2 roll-and-folds), then wrap and chill for 15 minutes. Roll and fold 5 more times (a total of 7), then the pastry is ready to use. Chill for 30 minutes before rolling to its final shape, then chill again for 30 minutes.

When the pastry has been cut to shape, 'knock up' the edges with the blade of a sharp knife to separate the layers and ensure a good rise.

rough puff pastry

250 g plain flour

a pinch of salt

150 g unsalted butter, chilled

about 150 ml iced water

makes about 550 g pastry, enough to line a tart tin 30 cm diameter

Sift the flour and salt into a large bowl. Quickly cut the butter into small cubes, and add to the flour. Stir the butter into the flour with a round-bladed knife until evenly distributed.

Sprinkle the water over the surface, mixing in with the knife as you do so. Mix with the knife until the dough starts to come together in a messy lump. Tip onto a floured work surface. Knead lightly until it forms a streaky, rather lumpy ball. Flatten the ball with the palm of your hand, then wrap in clingfilm and chill for 30 minutes until firm.

Unwrap the pastry and roll and fold as in the previous recipe.

A great friend showed me how to do this. It is really easy – but the butter must be very hard. It is made in exactly the same way as rough puff pastry except that you freeze and grate the butter, then roll and fold the dough as quickly as you can. My friend swears that it is lighter made with margarine, but I prefer using butter.

cheat's rough puff pastry

250 g plain flour

a pinch of salt

150 g unsalted butter, frozen

about 150 ml iced water

makes about 500 g pastry, enough to line a loose-based tart tin 30 cm diameter

Sift the flour and salt into a large bowl.

Hold the butter with a tea towel and, using the large side of a box grater, quickly grate the butter into the flour. Stir the butter into the flour with a round-bladed knife until evenly distributed.

Sprinkle the water over the surface, then mix with the knife until the dough starts to come together in a messy lump.

Transfer to a floured work surface and knead lightly until it forms a streaky, rather lumpy ball. Flatten the ball with the palm of your hand. Wrap in clingfilm and chill for 30 minutes until firm.

Unwrap and roll out away from you into a rectangle 3 times longer than it is wide – no exact measurements are needed here, but it should be about 1 cm thick. Remove any excess flour with a pastry brush.

Lightly mark the pastry into 3 equal sections with a blunt knife. Fold the third closest to you up over the middle third, then bring the top third towards you over the folded two-thirds.

Make a finger mark in the pastry to indicate you have completed 1 roll, then fold. Rewrap and chill for 15 minutes. Repeat twice more (indenting each time with the number of roll-and-folds completed). Wrap and chill for 30 minutes.

Roll to the final shape, then chill for 30 minutes.

*This sweet almond pastry is made in both France and Italy. If it is
overworked, it is tough – but properly made, it is crisp and light. It
is almost impossible to roll out, so shape it into a sausage, wrap in
clingfilm and chill until firm. Slice into thin rounds and push into the
base of the tin, pressing all over to make an even base (see right).*

my just-push-it-in pastry or pâte frolle (almond pastry)

200 g plain flour

a pinch of salt

75 g caster or icing sugar

75 g ground almonds

75 g unsalted butter, cubed, at room temperature

2 medium egg yolks

1/2 teaspoon real vanilla essence

2–3 tablespoons iced water

makes about 450 g pastry, enough to line a tart tin 23–25 cm diameter

Classic Method

Sift flour, salt and sugar into a mound on a clean work surface. Sprinkle the almonds on top of the flour. Make a well in the middle with your fist.

Put the butter, egg yolks and vanilla essence in the well. Using the fingers of one hand, 'peck' the eggs and butter together until the mixture resembles creamy scrambled eggs.

Flick the flour over the egg mixture and chop it through with a palette knife, until it is almost amalgamated but still very lumpy. Sprinkle with the water and chop again. Bring together quickly with your hands and knead lightly, then shape into a thick sausage. Wrap in clingfilm and chill for at least 2 hours.

Unwrap and cut into thin slices. Push the slices into the base and sides of the tin, overlapping them very slightly and pushing together so that they form an even layer. Chill or freeze for at least 30 minutes.

Food Processor Method

This method makes the whole process much easier. It keeps the pastry cool – useful on a hot day, or if you have hot hands.

Sift the flour and salt onto a sheet of greaseproof paper, then add the almonds.

Put the sugar, butter, egg yolks and vanilla in a food processor and blend until smooth. Add the water and blend again. Add the flour and salt mixture and pulse until everything is just combined. Transfer to a lightly floured work surface and proceed as in the classic method.

using filo pastry

Filo is a paper-thin, almost see-through pastry from Greece. It is sold fresh or frozen in sheets rolled up in a packet. Look for the authentic Greek filo rather than supermarket own brands, which tend to be thicker and coarser.

The important thing to remember when using filo pastry is not to let it dry out. Once it dries out, it cracks and is impossible to use. Always keep it in a plastic bag or under a slightly damp tea towel or sheet of clingfilm.

Cut all the pastry at once into the appropriate size and store in the plastic bag while you paint each sheet with melted butter to give it flavour and colour. Some people use olive oil, but I find butter is best. Use as soon as the pastry is buttered, whether filling, rolling, folding or pressing into a tart mould.

Filo is baked at 200°C (400°F) Gas 6 to set it, then turned down to 190°C (375°F) Gas 5 to finish and brown the pastry evenly. Don't cook it at a lower temperature or it will become soggy.

For a beautiful crisp tart shell, roll out the pastry as thinly as you dare. To combat shrinkage, chill or freeze the uncooked case before baking. Baking blind will ensure that the tart does not have a soggy base. Cook the filled base in the tin.

rolling out, lining a tart tin and baking blind

Preheat the oven to 200°C (400°F) Gas 6 – or 190°C (375°F) Gas 5 for pastries with a lot of sugar in them. (Ovens vary, so you may need slightly lower settings than these.) Roll out the pastry as thinly as necessary to line the dish you are using.

To line a tart tin, roll the flour-dusted pastry around the rolling pin to help you pick it up – this will avoid stretching the pastry, which might shrink during cooking. Lower the pastry over the tin and unroll to cover.

Use a small piece of pastry wrapped in clingfilm to help to push the pastry into the edges of the tin, then you can press the pastry up the sides of the tin.

Use the rolling pin to roll over the top – it will cut off any excess pastry very neatly. Alternatively, cut off the overhang with a very sharp knife. I also like to press the pastry into the flutes of the ring after I've cut off the excess, to give a good shape.

Prick the base all over with a fork, then chill or freeze for 15 minutes to set the pastry. Line with foil, baking parchment or all-purpose clingfilm (flicking the edges inwards towards the centre so that they don't catch on the pastry), then fill with baking beans.

Set on a baking sheet and bake blind in the preheated oven for 10–12 minutes. Remove the foil, baking parchment or clingfilm and the baking beans and return the tart shell to the oven for a further 5–7 minutes to dry out completely.

To stop it being soggy after filling and to fill any pricking holes, brush the hot or cold blind-baked case with beaten egg. Bake again for 5–10 minutes until set and shiny. If necessary, repeat the sealing process to make an impervious layer.

baking and freezing

Divide the pastry in half. Roll out each piece to about 3 mm thick. Line the tart tins, prick all over with a fork and chill or freeze for 15 minutes. Line with foil or all-purpose clingfilm and fill with baking beans.

For partial baking, bake at 200°C (400°F) Gas 6 for 10–12 minutes, or, **for full baking**, 15–18 minutes until just colouring around the edges. Remove the foil or clingfilm and beans (cool and reserve the beans for another day), then return the tart shells to the oven to dry out for 4–5 minutes until golden.

For freezing, divide the uncooked dough in half and form into flattened balls ready to thaw and roll out.

savoury tarts

Quiche Lorraine is a classic tart from Alsace and Lorraine, and the forerunner of many copies. Made well and with the best ingredients, this simplest of dishes is food fit for the gods. I like to add a little grated Gruyère to the filling.

quiche lorraine

1 recipe Basic Shortcrust Pastry (page 10) or Cheat's Rough Puff Pastry (page 18), chilled

200 g bacon lardons or cubed pancetta

5 medium eggs

200 ml double cream or crème fraîche

freshly grated nutmeg, to taste

50 g Gruyère cheese, grated

sea salt and freshly ground black pepper

a tart tin, 23 cm diameter

foil or baking parchment and baking beans

serves 4–6

If using basic shortcrust pastry, bring to room temperature. Preheat the oven to 200°C (400°F) Gas 6.

Roll out the pastry thinly on a lightly floured work surface and use to line the tart tin. Prick the base, chill or freeze for 15 minutes, then bake blind, following the method given on page 22.

Heat a non-stick frying pan, add the bacon, fry until brown and crisp, then drain on kitchen paper. Sprinkle over the base of the tart shell.

Put the eggs and cream in a bowl, beat well, and season with salt, pepper and nutmeg to taste. Carefully pour the mixture over the bacon and sprinkle with the Gruyère.

Bake for about 25 minutes until just set, golden brown and puffy. Serve warm or at room temperature.

There is nothing quite like the combination of meltingly soft sweet leeks, cream and pastry. This tart is perfect for a picnic served with some pâté and cold meats.

flamiche
(melting leek tart from belgium)

½ recipe Rich Shortcrust Pastry (page 10) or Pâte Brisée (page 15)*

75 g unsalted butter

900 g leeks, split, well washed and thickly sliced

1 teaspoon salt

4 medium egg yolks

300 ml double cream or crème fraîche

freshly grated nutmeg, to taste

sea salt and freshly ground black pepper

a tart tin, 20.5 cm diameter

a baking sheet

foil or baking parchment and baking beans

serves 4–6

Make the full amount and cook 2 tart shells, freezing 1 for later use.

Bring the pastry to room temperature. Preheat the oven to 200°C (400°F) Gas 6.

Roll out the pastry thinly on a lightly floured work surface, then use to line the tart tin. Prick the base, then chill or freeze for 15 minutes. Bake blind following the method on page 22.

Melt the butter in a large saucepan and add the leeks, stirring to coat. Add a few tablespoons of water and the 1 teaspoon salt, then cover with a lid. Steam very gently for at least 30 minutes (trying not to look too often), until soft and melting. Remove the lid and cook for a few minutes to evaporate any excess liquid – the mixture should be quite thick. Let cool.

Put the egg yolks and cream in a bowl, add salt, pepper and nutmeg to taste and beat well. Set the tart shell on a baking sheet. Spoon the cooled leeks evenly into the tart shell, fluffing them up a bit with a fork. Pour the eggs and cream mixture over the top.

Bake for 30 minutes or until set and pale golden brown. Serve warm.

Roquefort is a salty French blue cheese made from sheep's milk, but you could substitute any good-quality blue cheese. Walnuts are the perfect partner for blue cheese, especially when combined with the sweetly toasted slivers of garlic in this dressing.

roquefort tart
with walnut and toasted garlic dressing

1 recipe Pâte Brisée (page 15)

225 g cream or curd cheese (such as Philadelphia)

150 ml crème fraîche or double cream

3 medium eggs, beaten

175 g Roquefort or other good blue cheese

freshly ground black pepper

freshly grated nutmeg, to taste

3 tablespoons chopped fresh chives

walnut and toasted garlic dressing

3 garlic cloves

2 tablespoons olive oil

75 g walnut halves

1 tablespoon walnut oil

3 tablespoons chopped fresh parsley

a loose-based tart tin, 25 cm diameter

foil or baking parchment and baking beans

serves 6

Bring the pastry to room temperature. Preheat the oven to 200°C (400°F) Gas 6.

Roll out the pastry thinly on a lightly floured work surface, then use to line the tart tin. Prick the base, chill or freeze for 15 minutes, then bake blind following the method on page 22.

To make the filling, put the cream in a bowl and beat until softened. Beat in the crème fraîche and eggs. Crumble in the Roquefort and mix gently. Season with lots of black pepper and nutmeg. The cheese is salty, so you won't have to add extra salt. Stir in the chives and set aside.

Let the tart shell cool slightly and lower the oven to 190°C (375°F) Gas 5. Pour the filling into the case and bake for 30–35 minutes or until puffed and golden brown.

Meanwhile, to make the walnut and garlic dressing, slice the garlic into the thinnest of slivers. Heat the olive oil in a frying pan and add the garlic and walnuts. Stir-fry until the garlic is golden and the walnuts browned. Stir in the walnut oil and parsley.

Serve the tart warm or at room temperature with the warm walnut and garlic dressing.

This light, creamy, open tart is easy to make because there is no need to line a tin or bake blind – simply roll out the pastry and top like a pizza. Goats' cheese and walnuts are a great combination, especially when combined with soft, earthy leeks.

goats' cheese, leek and walnut tart

½ recipe Classic Puff Pastry (page 16), Rough Puff Pastry (page 17), Cheat's Rough Puff Pastry (page 18) or 250 g frozen puff pastry, thawed

50 g unsalted butter

4 small leeks, trimmed and sliced

1 teaspoon sea salt

200 g goats' cheese log with rind, sliced

olive oil, for sprinkling

sea salt and freshly ground black pepper

extra chopped fresh parsley, to serve

walnut paste

125 g walnut pieces

3 garlic cloves, crushed

6 tablespoons walnut oil

3 tablespoons chopped fresh parsley

a 28 cm dinner plate

a baking sheet

serves 4–6

Preheat the oven to 200°C (400°F) Gas 6. Roll out the pastry thinly on a lightly floured work surface and cut out a 28 cm circle using a dinner plate as a template. Set on a baking sheet and chill or freeze for at least 15 minutes.

Melt the butter in a large saucepan and add the leeks, stirring to coat. Add a few tablespoons of water and 1 teaspoon salt, then cover with a lid. Steam very gently for at least 20 minutes (trying not to look too often), until almost soft. Remove the lid and cook for a few minutes to evaporate any excess liquid. Let cool.

To make the walnut paste, blend the walnuts and garlic in a food processor with 2 tablespoons water. Beat in the walnut oil and stir in the parsley. Spread this mixture over the pastry, avoiding the rim.

Spoon the leeks into the pastry base and top with the slices of goats' cheese. Dot with any remaining walnut paste. Season with salt and freshly ground black pepper and sprinkle with olive oil. Bake for 20 minutes until the pastry is golden and the cheese bubbling and brown.

Sprinkle with more parsley and serve immediately.

Note If using one of the homemade puff pastries, make the full recipe and freeze the remainder for later use.

Tiny tartlets are great to serve at a drinks party. They look stunning and have a secret pocket of feta cheese lurking in the creamy, herby filling under the tomatoes. Make a double quantity of tomatoes – they keep well in the refrigerator and are great in salads.

slow-roasted tomato and herb tartlets with feta

1 recipe Rich Shortcrust Pastry (page 10) or Pâte Brisée (page 15), at room temperature

slow-roasted tomatoes

12–15 large ripe cherry tomatoes

2 garlic cloves, finely chopped

1 tablespoon dried oregano

4 tablespoons olive oil

sea salt and freshly ground black pepper

herby cheese filling

80 g full-fat soft cheese with garlic and herbs, such as Boursin

1 large egg, beaten

150 ml double cream

4 tablespoons chopped fresh mixed herbs, such as parsley, basil, marjoram or chives

75 g feta cheese

sea salt and freshly ground black pepper

tiny sprigs of thyme or cut chives, to serve

a plain biscuit cutter, 6 cm diameter

2 mini muffin tins, 12 holes each

foil or baking parchment and baking beans

makes 24 tartlets

Preheat the oven to 200°C (400°F) Gas 6. Roll out the pastry as thinly as possible on a lightly floured work surface. Use the biscuit cutter to stamp out 24 circles. Line the muffin tin holes with the pastry circles, then prick the bases and chill or freeze for 15 minutes. Bake blind following the method on page 22, then remove from the tins and let cool. Turn the oven down to 160°C (325°F) Gas 3.

Cut the tomatoes in half around the middle. Arrange cut side up on a baking sheet. Put the chopped garlic, oregano, olive oil, salt and lots of pepper in a bowl and mix well, then spoon or brush over the cut tomatoes. Bake slowly in the oven for about 1½–2 hours, checking every now and then. They should be slightly shrunken and still a brilliant red – if too dark, they will taste bitter.

Put the soft cheese in a bowl, add the egg, cream and herbs and beat until smooth. Season well. Cut the feta into 24 small cubes that will fit inside the tart shells.

When ready to bake, set the cases on a baking sheet, put a cube of feta in each one and top up with the garlic and herb mixture. Bake in the preheated oven at 180°C (350°F) Gas 4 for 15–20 minutes or until the filling is set. Top each with a tomato half, a sprinkle of the cooking juices and a thyme sprig or chive stem. Serve warm.

Notes
• The tart shells will keep for up to 1 week in an airtight container, but reheat to crisp them up before filling.
• Use the tomatoes immediately or pack into a storage jar and cover with olive oil.

The combination of creamy aubergine, garlic and tomatoes sings of the sun. This is the perfect tart to eat on a hot summer's day, accompanied by a bitter leafy salad and a lot of warm chatter.

creamy aubergine tart
with roasted cherry tomatoes

paprika and gruyère pastry

75 g unsalted butter

175 g plain flour

1/2 teaspoon sweet paprika

1/2 teaspoon dry mustard powder

55 g freshly grated Gruyère cheese

1 medium egg yolk

2 tablespoons iced water

sea salt and freshly ground black pepper

slow-roasted tomatoes

500 g large ripe cherry tomatoes

2 garlic cloves, finely chopped

1 tablespoon dried oregano

4 tablespoons olive oil

sea salt and freshly ground black pepper

aubergine filling

2 medium aubergines

2 garlic cloves, crushed

1/2 teaspoon smoked sweet paprika

1 tablespoon dried oregano

3 medium eggs, beaten

sea salt and freshly ground black pepper

2–3 tablespoons olive oil, to finish

a baking sheet

a loose-based rectangular tart tin, 25 x 15 cm

foil or baking parchment and baking beans

serves 6

To prepare the tomatoes, preheat the oven to 160°C (325°F) Gas 3. Cut the tomatoes in half around the middle and put them cut side up on a baking sheet.

Put the garlic, oregano, olive oil, salt and pepper in a bowl and mix well. Spoon or brush over the cut tomatoes. Bake slowly in the oven for about 2 hours, checking every now and then. They should be slightly shrunken and still a brilliant red colour – if too dark, they will taste bitter. (You can use the tomatoes straight away or pack into a jar and cover with olive oil.)

To make the pastry, rub the butter into the flour until it resembles fine breadcrumbs. Stir in the paprika, mustard, Gruyère, salt and pepper. Beat the egg with 2 tablespoons cold water and mix into the flour to make a soft dough. (Sprinkle with a little more water if the mixture is too dry.) Knead until smooth, wrap in clingfilm and chill for 30 minutes.

Roll out the pastry on a floured work surface and use to line the tart tin, then prick the base and chill or freeze for 15 minutes. Preheat the oven to 200°C (400°F) Gas 6 and bake blind following the method given on page 22. To make the filling, prick the aubergines all over and bake in the oven for 45 minutes, or until soft. Remove from the oven and let cool. (Or prick each aubergine in 2–3 places and microwave on HIGH for 12 minutes until soft.)

Turn down the oven to 180°C (350°F) Gas 4. Halve the aubergines and scoop out the flesh into a food processor. Add the garlic, paprika, oregano, eggs and salt and pepper to taste, then blend until smooth. Pour into the tart shell and bake for about 25 minutes or until set.

Remove from the oven and let cool. Arrange the roasted tomatoes over the surface to cover completely. Sprinkle with the olive oil (or use oil from the jar if you have stored the tomatoes), then serve.

Wickedly creamy, this tart puffs up in the oven, and is filled with the spring flavours of fresh asparagus and dill.

chunky new potato and asparagus tart

1 recipe Dill and Nutmeg Pastry (page 13)

500 g small new potatoes (or other waxy potatoes)

400 g fresh asparagus

4 large eggs, plus 2 yolks, beaten

150 ml crème fraîche

sea salt and freshly ground black pepper

a little olive oil, to serve

a rectangular tart tin, 20 x 28 cm

a baking sheet

foil or baking parchment and baking beans

serves 6–8

Bring the pastry to room temperature. Preheat the oven to 200°C (400°F) Gas 6.

Roll out the pastry thinly on a lightly floured work surface, then use to line the tart tin. Prick the base, chill or freeze for 15 minutes, then bake blind following the method given on page 22.

Reduce the heat to 190°C (375°F) Gas 5. Meanwhile, boil the potatoes in salted water for 20 minutes until tender. While boiling, trim the asparagus and cut into 4 cm lengths. Reserve the tips. Add the asparagus stems to the potatoes 6 minutes before the potatoes are cooked.

Drain and refresh the vegetables in cold water, then thickly slice the potatoes. Put the eggs and crème fraîche in a bowl, whisk well, then season with salt and pepper.

Arrange the potatoes and asparagus over the base of the tart shell and pour in the egg mixture. Set on a baking sheet and bake in the preheated oven for 25–30 minutes until puffed up and golden brown.

Meanwhile, cook the reserved asparagus tips in boiling salted water until tender, then drain and refresh. Toss the tips in a little olive oil and serve a spoonful with each portion. Serve warm.

Large dark mushrooms are full of flavour – the darker, the better. This tart has a creamy filling laced with tarragon and lemon. The garlicky, crunchy topping turns it into a giant version of a stuffed mushroom – but more sophisticated. Serve with a fresh tomato salad.

dark mushroom and tarragon tart

1 recipe Cheese Shortcrust Pastry (page 13)

75 g unsalted butter

1 onion, sliced

500 g dark open mushrooms, sliced

freshly squeezed juice of 1 lemon

2 tablespoons chopped fresh tarragon

200 g mascarpone cheese, softened

3 large eggs, beaten

sea salt and freshly ground black pepper

garlic crunch topping

55 g unsalted butter

150 g stale breadcrumbs

3 garlic cloves, chopped

finely grated zest of 1 unwaxed lemon

3 tablespoons chopped fresh parsley

a deep fluted tart tin, 25 cm diameter

foil or baking parchment and baking beans

serves 6–8

Bring the pastry to room temperature. Preheat the oven to 200°C (400°F) Gas 6.

Roll out the pastry thinly on a lightly floured work surface. Use to line the tart tin, then chill or freeze for 15 minutes and bake blind following the method given on page 22.

Melt the butter in a frying pan, add the onion and fry until soft and golden. Add the mushrooms, lemon juice, salt and pepper, then fry over medium heat for 5 minutes until the mushrooms are tender and the liquid has evaporated. Stir in the tarragon, then let the mixture cool slightly.

To make the topping, melt the butter in a frying pan, add the breadcrumbs, garlic, lemon zest and parsley and fry over brisk heat until the breadcrumbs begin to crisp but not colour too much. Tip the mixture into a bowl.

Put the mascarpone and eggs in a bowl and beat well. Stir in the mushroom mixture. Pour into the tart shell, then sprinkle with the topping and bake for 20–25 minutes until set, crisp and golden on top. Serve warm.

This Provençal version of Italian pizza is seen in every boulangerie in the Midi. There are many variations, and I've distilled them here into one perfect picnic food.

pissaladière
(provençal tomato and onion pizza)

yeast pastry

10 g fresh yeast

a pinch of sugar

200 g plain flour

55 g unsalted butter, chilled and cubed

1 medium egg, beaten

a pinch of salt

olive oil, for greasing

herby onion filling

3 tablespoons olive oil

1.5 kg mild onions, thinly sliced

3 garlic cloves, chopped

2 teaspoons dried herbes de Provence

tomato sauce

800 g canned chopped tomatoes

3 tablespoons tomato purée

2 tablespoons olive oil

1 teaspoon harissa (chilli-spice paste)

150 ml white wine

sea salt and freshly ground black pepper

to finish

15 anchovy fillets in oil, halved lengthways

olive oil, for sprinkling

18 very good black olives

a Swiss roll tin, 33 x 20 cm

serves 6

To make the onion filling, heat the oil in a large saucepan, add the onions and garlic and 3 tablespoons water. Cover and cook over gentle heat for about 1 hour or until meltingly soft, but not coloured. Stir the onions occasionally and watch they do not burn. Stir in the herbs, then set a sieve over a bowl and tip the onions into the sieve. Reserve the caught juices for the yeast pastry.

To make the pastry, cream the fresh yeast and sugar in a bowl, then whisk in 3 tablespoons of the reserved onion liquid. Leave for 10 minutes until frothy.

Sift the flour into a bowl and rub in the butter. Make a well in the centre and add the egg, yeast mixture and salt. Mix until it starts to come together, then transfer to a floured work surface and knead until smooth. Oil the bowl. Return the dough to the oiled bowl and put the bowl inside a polythene bag. Let the dough rise for about 1 hour or until doubled in size.

To make the tomato sauce, put all the ingredients in a saucepan, mix well and bring to the boil. Simmer uncovered for about 1 hour, stirring occasionally until well reduced and very thick. Season well and set aside.

Preheat the oven to 190°C (375°F) Gas 5. Punch down the dough, knead, then roll out onto a lightly floured surface. Use to line the Swiss roll tin, bringing the dough well up the edges.

Spread the tomato sauce over the base and cover with the onions. Arrange the anchovies in a lattice over the onions. Sprinkle with olive oil and bake for 1 hour until the pastry is golden and crisp. Dot with the olives and serve warm or at room temperature.

Note If using easy-blend dried yeast, mix 1 teaspoon with the flour, rub in the butter, then continue as the main recipe.

These delicate bites are as light as air, but packed with fresh Asian flavours. I like to use canned white crabmeat from the Pacific for these – not only does it taste very good, but there is no shell or messy bits to deal with if you're catering for a large number of people. It is also much cheaper than fresh.

spicy crab in filo cups

9 sheets filo pastry, about A4 paper size

50 g unsalted butter, melted

spicy crab filling

200 g canned white crabmeat in brine, drained

75 g canned water chestnuts, drained and finely chopped or sliced

3 cm fresh ginger, peeled and cut into fine strips

2 spring onions, trimmed and finely sliced

finely grated zest and juice of 1 unwaxed lime

1 garlic clove, crushed

½ fresh red chilli, deseeded and finely chopped

2 teaspoons sesame oil

2 tablespoons chopped fresh coriander

sea salt and freshly ground black pepper

3 mini muffin tins, 12 holes each, brushed with melted butter

makes about 36

Preheat the oven to 180°C (350°F) Gas 4.

Unroll the filo and cut the stack into 108 squares, each measuring 7 x 7 cm. To do this, keep the sheets stacked on top of each other, then mark the top sheet into 12 squares. Cut down through all the layers, giving 108 squares. Pile into 2–3 stacks and keep beside you in a plastic bag.

To make a filo cup, take 3 squares of filo, brush each with melted butter and lay one on top of the other, so that the points make a star, and do not touch each other. Quickly but gently press into one of the holes of the prepared muffin tin, so the points of the filo shoot upwards like a handkerchief. Repeat with all the remaining filo until you have 36 cups.

Bake in the oven for about 8–10 minutes until golden. Remove, let cool in the tin, then carefully remove to a tray (they are very fragile).

Put the crab in a bowl and fluff up with a fork. Stir in the water chestnuts, ginger and spring onions. Put the lime zest and juice in a separate bowl, add the crushed garlic, chilli and sesame oil, and season to taste. Stir into the crab mixture (this can be done up to 4 hours in advance), then stir in the coriander.

Fill the cups with the crab mixture just before serving (they can go a little soggy if they are kept too long).

The sweet and salty taste of fresh crab (if you can get it) mixed with mild red chillies pickled in sweet vinegar is fantastic. They seem made for each other. Serve this with an avocado salsa or just plain sliced avocado dressed with a coriander vinaigrette.

crab and sweet pickled chilli tart

1 recipe Cheese Shortcrust Pastry (page 13)

chilli crab filling

2 tablespoons olive oil

a bunch of spring onions, sliced

6 medium eggs

300 ml double cream

1 tablespoon Dijon mustard

500 g fresh or frozen white crabmeat, thawed and drained

8 mild, sweet pickled red chilli peppers, deseeded and roughly chopped

100 g freshly grated Parmesan

freshly ground black pepper

a loose-based tart tin, 25 cm diameter, 3 cm deep

a baking sheet

foil or baking parchment and baking beans

serves 6–8

Bring the pastry to room temperature. Preheat the oven to 200°C (400°F) Gas 6.

Roll out the pastry on a lightly floured work surface to a thickness of 3 mm and use to line the tart tin. Chill or freeze for 15 minutes, then bake blind following the method given on page 22. Let cool.

Reduce the heat to 180°C (350°F) Gas 4. Heat the olive oil in a pan and fry the spring onions until softened, but not coloured. Let cool slightly.

Put the eggs, cream and mustard in a bowl and whisk well. Stir in the crab, cooked spring onions, sweet chilli peppers and Parmesan, then season with plenty of black pepper. Spoon into the pastry shell and level the surface.

Set on a baking sheet and bake for about 45 minutes until just firm. Serve warm or at room temperature.

I make this tart extra special by blending in a little smoked salmon or gravadlax at the same time as the eggs and cream. This gives the tart a mysterious, slightly smoky flavour and a velvety texture.

salmon, dill and parmesan tart with pickled cucumber

1 recipe Rich Shortcrust Pastry (page 10) or Pâte Brisée (page 15)

salmon and dill filling

450 g fresh salmon fillets (with or without skin)

300 ml double cream

75 g smoked salmon pieces (scraps will do, but cut off any brown bits)

3 medium eggs, beaten

3 tablespoons chopped fresh dill

25 g freshly grated Parmesan cheese

sea salt and freshly ground black pepper

cucumber topping

2 large cucumbers

1 tablespoon sea salt

1 tablespoon caster sugar

100 ml white wine vinegar or cider vinegar

2 tablespoons chopped fresh dill

freshly ground white pepper

extra dill sprigs, to garnish

a tart tin, 25 cm diameter

a baking sheet

foil or baking parchment and baking beans

serves 6–8

Bring the pastry to room temperature. Preheat the oven to 200°C (400°F) Gas 6.

Roll out the pastry thinly on a lightly floured work surface, then use to line the tart tin. Chill or freeze for 15 minutes, then bake blind following the method on page 22. Remove from the oven and reduce the heat to 190°C (375°F) Gas 5.

Put the salmon fillets in a shallow pan and cover with cold water. Add a little salt and bring slowly to the boil. Just before the water boils, turn off the heat and leave the salmon in the water until it is cold – by then it will be cooked and very moist. Lift it out of the water and drain well. Peel off any skin and check for bones. Flake coarsely.

Put the cream in a blender, add the smoked salmon and eggs, then blend until smooth. Season well with salt and pepper and stir in the dill. Sprinkle the salmon flakes over the base of the tart and pour in the smoked salmon mixture. Sprinkle with the Parmesan, set on a baking sheet and bake in the preheated oven for 25 minutes, until just set. Remove from the oven and let cool completely.

Meanwhile, to make the cucumber topping, peel the cucumber, then slice thinly with a mandoline or a food processor. Spread in a colander and sprinkle with the salt, mixing well. Stand the colander on a plate and let drain for 30 minutes. Rinse well and squeeze out the excess moisture. Spread the cucumber on a large plate.

Dissolve the sugar in the vinegar and stir in the dill. Pour this over the cucumber and let marinate for at least 1 hour before serving.

To serve, drain the cucumber well and arrange it casually over the top of the salmon tart. Grind over lots of white pepper, top with dill sprigs, then serve immediately. Any extra salad can be served on the side.

Make these pretty little tartlets for a special occasion – they simply explode with fabulous flavours. I usually make them with smoked salmon, but use avruga (herring roe prepared like caviar) if you can find it – just perfect with the hidden sour cream and chives.

smoked salmon, vodka and sour cream aspic tartlets

250 g Rich Shortcrust Pastry (page 10) or Pâte Brisée (page 15)*

flavoured aspic

1 sheet of leaf gelatine

150 ml light fish stock

1–2 tablespoons lemon-flavoured vodka

2 tablespoons chopped fresh chives

smoked salmon filling

60 ml sour cream

90 g smoked salmon, chopped (or avruga or keta caviar)

whole chives, to garnish

a plain biscuit cutter, 6 cm diameter

2 mini muffin tins, 12 holes each

foil or baking parchment and baking beans

makes 24 tartlets

Make up the full amount and freeze the rest for later use.

Bring the pastry to room temperature. Preheat the oven to 200°C (400°F) Gas 6.

Roll out the pastry as thinly as possible on a lightly floured work surface, then stamp out 24 circles with the biscuit cutter. Use these to line the holes of the mini muffin tins. Prick the bases and chill or freeze for 15 minutes. Bake blind using the method given on page 22, remove from the tins and let cool.

To make the flavoured aspic, soak the leaf gelatine in cold water for 2–3 minutes until soft. Warm the fish stock, then stir in the drained gelatine until dissolved. Add the vodka. Let cool until syrupy but still pourable, then stir in the chives.

Arrange the tart shells on a tray and add ½ teaspoon sour cream to each tartlet. Cover with a mound of smoked salmon, then spoon in enough aspic to fill to the top of the pastry. Chill in the refrigerator for 15–20 minutes to set, then top each one with a couple of thin chive stems. Serve immediately.

Notes

• Leaf gelatine is best here, because it is flavourless. Powdered gelatine has a more defined taste, which can spoil the flavour of the fish. But if you do want to use it, use 1 level teaspoon. Take 3 tablespoons out of the stock and put it in a bowl or teacup. Sprinkle the gelatine over the liquid, let it swell for 10 minutes, then heat gently to let it dissolve. Stir into the remaining stock and use as above.

• You can keep the bases in an airtight container for up to 1 week, but reheat to crisp them up before filling.

This is a tart filled with uncooked lemon curd and baked in the oven until just firm. The recipe comes from my sister Jacks, who has a reputation for her fantastic lemon tarts. She makes really tiny ones for champagne receptions and weddings – if you are making bite-sized morsels, the pastry must be wonderfully thin so that they melt in the mouth.

classic lemon tart

1 recipe Sweet Rich Shortcrust Pastry (page 10), at room temperature

1 egg, beaten, to seal the pastry

crème fraîche, to serve (optional)

lemon filling

6 large eggs

350 g caster sugar

finely grated zest and strained juice of 4 juicy unwaxed lemons

125 g unsalted butter, melted

a loose-based fluted tart tin, 23 cm diameter

a baking sheet

serves 8

Preheat the oven to 190°C (375°F) Gas 5. Roll out the pastry thinly on a lightly floured work surface, and use to line the tart tin. Chill or freeze for 15 minutes, then bake blind following the method given on page 22. Brush with the beaten egg, then bake again for 5–10 minutes until set and shiny (this will prevent the filling making the pastry soggy). Reduce the heat to 150°C (300°F) Gas 2.

To make the filling, put the eggs, sugar, lemon zest and juice, and butter in a food processor and blend until smooth.

Set the baked tart shell on a baking sheet and pour in the filling. Bake in the heated oven for about 1 hour (it may need a little longer, depending on your oven), until just set. Remove from the oven and let cool completely.

Serve at room temperature, maybe with a spoonful of crème fraîche.

Note For a special occasion you can decorate this tart with shreds of candied lemon zest. Peel the zest only from 3–4 unwaxed lemons, leaving behind any white pith. Cut the zest into very fine shreds with a sharp knife. Make a sugar syrup by boiling 75 g caster sugar with 150 ml water. Stir in the shreds and simmer for about 10 minutes until tender and almost transparent. Carefully lift out of the syrup, drain, then sprinkle the shreds around the edge of the tart while still warm, to form a ring. Cool before serving.

sweet tarts

I have been making this tart since I started cooking at the tender age of eight – it used to be my 'pièce de résistance'. Blending the sugar with large peelings of lemon zest transfers all the essential oils to the sugar and gives a wonderful aroma. Using cottage cheese instead of cream cheese gives a lighter texture and will cut the calories.

simple lemon cheese tart

1 recipe Sweet Rich Shortcrust Pastry (page 10)

1 unwaxed lemon

75 g caster sugar

350 g cream cheese or full-fat soft cheese such as Philadelphia

1 medium egg, plus 3 egg yolks

2 teaspoons real vanilla essence

a loose-based tart tin, 23 cm diameter

serves 4–6

Bring the pastry to room temperature. Preheat the oven to 190°C (375°F) Gas 5.

Roll out the pastry on a lightly floured work surface and use to line the tart tin. Prick the base, then chill or freeze for 15 minutes. Bake blind following the method given on page 22. Let cool.

Peel the zest from the lemon leaving any white pith behind, then squeeze the juice. Put the zest and sugar in a food processor or small blender, and process until the mixture looks damp.

Add the lemon juice and blend again – the lemon zest should be completely dissolved into the sugar. Add the cheese, whole egg and egg yolks and vanilla essence. Blend until smooth and pour into the baked case.

Bake for about 25 minutes until just set and lightly browned on top. Remove from the oven and let cool. Serve at room temperature.

This unusual chocolate and almond biscuit crust is the perfect foil for a sharp lemon and almond filling.

lemon and almond tart with chocolate amaretti crust

250 g amaretti biscuits or Italian ratafias

50 g dark chocolate, grated or chopped

75 g unsalted butter, melted

lemon almond filling

3 unwaxed lemons

4 large eggs

120 g sugar

120 g unsalted butter, melted

120 g ground almonds

150 g crème fraîche

a deep tart tin,
23 cm diameter, 3 cm deep

a baking sheet

serves 6–8

Preheat the oven to 180°C (350°F) Gas 4.

Put the amaretti biscuits in a food processor and blend until finely crushed. Add the chocolate and blend again. Pour in the melted butter and blend until well mixed and coming together.

Put the tart tin onto a baking sheet. Press the mixture evenly over the base and sides of the tart tin (a potato masher and the back of a small spoon will help). Bake for 10 minutes to set the base. Remove from the oven and press the puffed-up crust down again.

Finely grate the zest from the lemons and squeeze and strain the juice. Beat the eggs in a bowl and whisk in the lemon zest and juice, sugar, melted butter and ground almonds. Pour into the amaretti case and bake for 25 minutes until set and very lightly brown on top.

Cool, then spread with the crème fraîche and serve at room temperature.

In these delicious little tarts, the zesty lemon meringue puffs up like a cloud over a sea of blueberries, then sets to a feather-light cooked mousse. Irresistible!

blueberry and lemon cloud tartlets

1 recipe Pâte Brisée (page 15)

500 g fresh blueberries, plus extra to serve

icing sugar, to dust

crème fraîche, to serve

lemon filling

4 large eggs, separated

150 g caster sugar

finely grated zest of 2 lemons or 3 limes

freshly squeezed juice of 1 lemon or 2 limes

a pinch of salt

8 tartlet tins, 10 cm diameter

a baking sheet

makes 8 tartlets

Bring the pastry to room temperature. Preheat the oven to 200°C (400°F) Gas 6.

Roll out the pastry on a lightly floured work surface, then use to line the tartlet tins. Prick the bases and chill or freeze for 15 minutes. bake blind following the method given on page 22. Lower the oven to 160°C (325°F) Gas 3.

Whisk the egg yolks and 75 g of the sugar with an electric beater until the mixture is pale and mousse-like, and leaves a trail when the beaters are lifted. Whisk in the lemon zest and juice. Set the bowl over a saucepan of simmering water and stir the mixture until thickened enough to coat the back of a wooden spoon. Let cool.

Whisk the egg whites with the salt until soft peaks form, then gradually whisk in the remaining sugar, a spoonful at a time. Beat a spoonful of the egg white mixture into the lemon mixture to loosen it, then carefully fold in the remainder.

Put a single layer of blueberries in each tartlet case. Carefully cover with spoonfuls of the lemon mousse, making sure the mousse seals the edges. Put onto the baking sheet and bake for 15–20 minutes until beginning to rise. Dust with icing sugar and return to the oven for 4–5 minutes until just beginning to brown.

Serve warm (the tartlets will sink a little) or at room temperature with spoonfuls of crème fraîche and extra blueberries.

The combination of blueberries and lime is terrific, especially when laced with the herby notes of Drambuie. I first tasted wild blueberries sprinkled with Drambuie while fishing in the lochs of Scotland – it was manna from heaven.

blueberry and lime sour cream pie

1 recipe Pâte Brisée (page 15)

300 ml sour cream

2 tablespoons freshly squeezed lime juice

2 tablespoons Drambuie or other whisky liqueur

100 g caster sugar

$^1/_4$ teaspoon ground cinnamon

$^1/_4$ teaspoon ground allspice

a pinch of salt

2 large eggs, beaten

450 g fresh blueberries

100 ml lime marmalade

a deep tart tin, 22 cm diameter, 3 cm deep

a baking sheet

serves 6

Bring the pastry to room temperature. Preheat the oven to 200°C (400°F) Gas 6.

Roll out the pastry thinly on a lightly floured work surface, then use to line the tart tin. Prick the base, then chill or freeze for 15 minutes. Bake blind following the method on page 22.

Lower the oven to 180°C (350°F) Gas 4. Put the sour cream, fresh lime juice, Drambuie, sugar, spices, salt and eggs in a bowl and mix well. Put a single layer of blueberries in the tart shell and pour over the sour cream mixture.

Put the baking sheet in the oven to heat. Bake the tart on the preheated sheet for 45 minutes until the filling is set and the pastry cooked. Remove from the oven and let cool. Remove from the tart tin.

Melt the marmalade and, when runny, strain through a sieve. Mix the rest of the blueberries with the marmalade and pile on top of the cooled pie. Chill for at least 1 hour, but remove from the refrigerator 15 minutes before serving.

I make these for special teatime treats in the summer, when Scottish strawberries are in season. They beat anything you can buy from the baker or supermarket. Brushing the inside of the tart shells with chocolate keeps the pastry crisp and adds a new dimension to the traditional strawberry tart.

strawberry chocolate tarts

1 recipe Sweet Rich Shortcrust Pastry (page 10)

200 g plain chocolate, to make swirls and brush the tart shells

mascarpone filling

250 g mascarpone cheese

2 tablespoons caster sugar

250 g fromage frais or curd cheese

rosewater or Grand Marnier, to taste

strawberry topping

12 large, ripe strawberries

redcurrant jelly, for brushing

a biscuit cutter, 10 cm diameter

12 deep fluted tart or brioche tins, 8 cm diameter

non-stick baking parchment

makes 12 small deep tarts

Bring the pastry to room temperature. Preheat the oven to 190°C (375°F) Gas 5.

Roll out the pastry as thinly as possible on a lightly floured work surface, then cut out 12 circles with the biscuit cutter. Use to line 6 of the tart tins.

Trim the edges and prick the bases. Then set another tin inside each one – this will weight down the pastry while it is baking. Chill or freeze for 15 minutes. Bake blind for 10–12 minutes until golden and set. Remove the inner tins and return to the oven to dry out for 5 minutes. Cool, then remove from the outer tins. Repeat with the remaining pastry to make another 6.

Melt the chocolate and sprinkle spoonfuls randomly from a height onto non-stick baking parchment. Let cool until set. Use the remaining chocolate to brush the insides of the tarts, making sure they are completely covered. Let cool and set.

To make the filling, put the mascarpone and sugar in a bowl and beat until creamy, then beat in the fromage frais. Add rosewater to taste.

Spoon this mixture into the tartlets, filling well, then sit a nice fat strawberry on top. Melt the redcurrant jelly, cool slightly, then brush over the strawberries and the exposed mascarpone surface. Set aside in a cool place to set.

To serve, break up the set chocolate swirls and push a shard into each tart. Serve immediately.

A tart that celebrates the perfect marriage of raspberries and cream. This is simplicity itself to make, but must be assembled at the last moment to keep the freshness and crispness of the pastry. I like to sweeten the cream with a little sieved homemade raspberry jam and I add a dash of framboise (raspberry liqueur) if I have it.

fresh raspberry tart

1 recipe Pâte Brisée (page 15)

2–3 tablespoons homemade raspberry jam

600 ml double cream, or 300 ml double cream mixed with 300 ml crème fraîche

2 tablespoons framboise (optional)

750 g fresh raspberries

150 ml raspberry or redcurrant jelly (any berry jelly will do)

a loose-based fluted tart tin, 20.5 cm diameter

serves 6–8

Bring the pastry to room temperature. Preheat the oven to 200°C (400°F) Gas 6.

Roll out the pastry thinly on a lightly floured work surface, and use to line the tart tin. Prick the base, chill or freeze for 15 minutes. then bake blind following the method given on page 22. Let cool.

Press the raspberry jam through a sieve to remove the seeds, then put in a large bowl. Add the cream and framboise if using. Whisk until thick and just holding peaks. Spoon into the tart case and level the surface. Cover with the raspberries, arranging a final neat layer on top.

Put the raspberry jelly in a small saucepan and warm it gently until liquid. Brush over the raspberries to glaze. Put in the refrigerator to chill and set for 10 minutes only before serving (no longer or the tart will become soggy).

Note You may like to brush the inside of the tart shell with melted white chocolate before filling – this will keep the pastry crisp, and make the tart even more of a special treat. You could also decorate the top with white chocolate curls (use a chocolate with a low cocoa solid content, bring it to room temperature first, then shave with a potato peeler).

Variation I sometimes lightly toss the raspberries in the jelly (you may need a bit of extra jelly to do this), coating them completely without breaking them. I then spoon them over the surface in a higgledy-piggledy fashion.

Another French pâtisserie classic. The secret of this tart is patience and neatness, because it just has to look beautiful. Make it with the juiciest apples you can – Golden Delicious are very good. The pastry provides a firm, crisp support. Unsweetened pâte brisée is used here, because the tart has to be baked for a long time and pastries with a high sugar content would scorch before the apples were cooked.

tarte aux pommes
(french apple tart)

1 recipe Pâte Brisée (page 15)

apple filling

4–5 well-flavoured dessert apples, peeled and cored

3 tablespoons caster sugar

50 g unsalted butter, cubed

4–6 tablespoons apricot jam

2 tablespoons Calvados (apple brandy) or brandy

a loose-based tart tin, 25 cm diameter

a baking sheet

serves 6–8

Bring the pastry to room temperature. Preheat the oven to 200°C (400°F) Gas 6 and put a baking sheet in the oven to heat.

Roll out the pastry thinly on a lightly floured work surface and use to line the tart tin. Chill or freeze for 15 minutes.

Meanwhile, slice the apples thinly, and coarsely chop up the uneven smaller pieces. Arrange these smaller pieces in the base of the tart. Cover with one-third of the slices any way you like. Arrange the remaining slices neatly in concentric rings over the chopped apples. Sprinkle with the sugar and dot with the butter.

Set the tart tin on the baking sheet and bake in the preheated oven for 1 hour, or until the apples are very well browned and the pastry golden. Remove from the oven and transfer to a cooling rack. Wait for 5 minutes, then remove the tart tin.

Put the apricot jam and Calvados in a small saucepan and warm gently. Strain, then use to glaze the apples. Serve at room temperature.

This familiar favourite is easy to make – and a must for anyone with a young family. The fruit filling is not too spicy, and children will love the crumble topping.

lemony apple crumble tart

1 recipe Basic Shortcrust Pastry (page 10) or Sweet Rich Shortcrust Pastry (page 10)

custard, to serve

crumble topping

75 g all-purpose flour

75 g demerara sugar

75 g unsalted butter, softened

finely grated zest of 1 unwaxed lemon

spiced apple filling

6 large Cox's Orange Pippins or Granny Smiths, peeled and cored

55 g sultanas

finely grated zest and juice of 1 unwaxed lemon

55 g soft brown sugar

$1/2$ teaspoon ground cinnamon

$1/4$ teaspoon freshly grated nutmeg

1 tablespoon each all-purpose flour and caster sugar, mixed

a tart tin, 23 cm diameter

serves 6

Bring the pastry to room temperature. Preheat the oven to 200°C (400°F) Gas 6, or 190°C (375°F) Gas 5 if using sweet rich shortcrust pastry.

Roll out the pastry on a lightly floured work surface, and use to line the tart tin. Prick the base, then chill or freeze for 15 minutes. Bake blind following the method given on page 22. Let cool.

To make the topping, put the flour, sugar, butter and lemon zest in a bowl and rub lightly between your fingers until the mixture resembles fine breadcrumbs. Chill in the refrigerator until needed.

To make the apple filling, chop the apples into small chunks, put in a bowl and toss with the sultanas, lemon zest and juice, sugar and spices. Sprinkle the base of the tart shell with the flour and caster sugar, then arrange the apples on top.

Sprinkle the crumble mixture over the apples. Bake for 15 minutes, then reduce the heat to 180°C (350°F) Gas 4 and bake for another 30 minutes. Serve warm with custard.

A tart named after the Tatin sisters who, as legend has it, created an upside-down apple tart by mistake. The type of apple used is crucial – it must retain its shape during cooking and yet have a good flavour. I like to use Cox's Orange Pippins, Golden Delicious or Jonagolds.

tarte des demoiselles tatin

1 recipe Rough Puff Pastry (page 17) or Cheat's Rough Puff Pastry (page 18) or 450 g frozen puff pastry, thawed

300 g sugar

150 g chilled unsalted butter, thinly sliced

about 2.5 kg evenly sized dessert apples

crème fraîche or whipped cream, to serve

non-stick baking parchment

a baking sheet

a flameproof cast-iron frying pan or tarte Tatin pan, 28 cm diameter

serves 6

Preheat the oven to 190°C (375°F) Gas 5.

Roll out the pastry on non-stick baking parchment to a circle about 30 cm in diameter, slide onto a baking sheet and chill. Sprinkle the sugar over the base of the frying pan or tarte Tatin pan. Cover with the sliced butter.

Peel, halve and core the apples. Add the apple halves to the outside edge of the pan – set the first one at an angle, almost on its edge, then arrange the others all around the edge so that they slightly overlap and butt up against each other. Add another ring of apples inside, so that the pan is almost filled, then add a whole half to fill the gap in the centre. The apples should now cover the entire surface of the pan. They look awkward and bulky, but will cook down and meld together later.

Put the pan over gentle heat and cook for about 45 minutes until the sugar and butter have caramelized and the apples have softened underneath. (Check from time to time and adjust the heat if necessary. The juices will gradually bubble up the sides; keep cooking until they are a dark amber.)

Lay the pastry over the apples in the pan and tuck the edges down into the pan, to make the rim of the tart. Prick the top of the pastry here and there with a fork, then set the pan on the baking sheet. Bake in the preheated oven for 25–30 minutes until the pastry is risen and golden.

Remove the pan from the oven and immediately invert the tart onto a warm serving plate (watch out for hot caramel). Replace any apple slices that stick to the pan. Serve warm, not hot, with crème fraîche.

What could be better than the simplicity of pears poached in red wine? This tart fits the bill. The pears absorb the deep flavour of the wine and turn a fabulously rich colour. If you want to be outrageously extravagant, use Italian Vin Santo or Marsala instead of wine and cut down on the sugar – the pears will turn a beautiful dark mahogany.

drunken pear tart

1 recipe Pâte Brisée (page 15) or Cheat's Rough Puff Pastry (page 18)

8 under-ripe medium pears

1 cinnamon stick

75 g caster sugar

600 ml full-bodied red wine

slivered pistachios or almonds, to finish

crème fraîche or whipped cream, to serve

a cast-iron frying pan, 25 cm diameter

serves 6

If using pâte brisée, bring to room temperature before rolling out.

Peel the pears, halve lengthways and carefully scoop out the core with a teaspoon or melon baller. Arrange them around the base of the frying pan in concentric circles, wide ends outwards and the points facing into the centre. Any pears remaining should be cut up and used to fill any gaps.

Crumble the cinnamon over the top and sprinkle with the sugar. Carefully pour in the red wine, then bring to the boil. Cover and simmer gently for about 1 hour or until tender.

Preheat the oven to 200°C (400°F) Gas 6. Uncover the pan and hold a plate or pan lid over the pears to hold them back while you pour off the juices into a saucepan. Boil the juices hard until well reduced and syrupy, then sprinkle back over the pears.

Roll out the pastry on a lightly floured work surface to a circle slightly larger than the diameter of the pan. Lift the pastry over the pears and tuck the edge of the pastry down into the pan. Bake for about 35–40 minutes until the pastry is crisp and golden.

As soon as it is ready, invert the tart onto a plate or it will stick – the fruit will be very hot, so be careful you don't burn your fingers. Sprinkle with the pistachios and serve warm or at room temperature, with a good deal of crème fraîche.

The original version of this tart is sold at my local pâtisserie in France. Monsieur Demont makes all his own pastry on the premises, and when peaches are in season and at their best, these tarts appear in the window in all their rustic glory. So simple and so good – especially with all-butter homemade pastry.

free-form caramelized peach tart

1 recipe Classic Puff Pastry (page 16), Rough Puff Pastry (page 17) or Cheat's Rough Puff Pastry (page 18)

4–6 ripe peaches

55 g unsalted butter

freshly squeezed juice of ½ lemon

150 g caster sugar

whipped cream or crème fraîche, to serve

a dinner plate, 28 cm diameter (to use as a template)

a baking sheet

serves 6

Preheat the oven to 230°C (450°F) Gas 8.

Roll out the pastry on a lightly floured work surface and cut out a circle 28 cm diameter, using a large dinner plate as a template. Lift onto a baking sheet and make an edge by twisting the pastry over itself all the way around. Press lightly to seal. Still on the baking sheet, chill or freeze for at least 15 minutes.

Peel the peaches if necessary, then halve and pit them and cut into chunky slices. Put the butter in a saucepan, then add the lemon juice and half the sugar. Heat until melted, then add the peaches and toss gently. Pile the peaches all over the pastry in a casual way. Sprinkle with the remaining sugar and bake in the preheated oven for 20–25 minutes until golden, puffed and caramelized. Serve with whipped cream.

The rich, buttery brioche pastry contains a set golden custard studded with fresh cherries. This is one of those moreish pastries best served in thin slices with a cup of tea or coffee.

golden custard and cherry brioche tart

brioche pastry

2 teaspoons active dried yeast*

4 tablespoons milk, warmed

15 g caster sugar

250 g strong all-purpose flour

1 teaspoon salt

2 large eggs, at room temperature

180 g unsalted butter, softened

custard and cherry filling

200 ml milk

100 ml double cream

1 vanilla pod, split

2 large eggs, plus 1 egg yolk

125 g caster or vanilla sugar

3 tablespoons all-purpose flour

350 g fresh cherries, pitted

extra beaten egg, to glaze

a rectangular loose-based tart tin, 33 x 9.5 cm

serves 6

*To use easy-blend dried yeast, mix 1 teaspoon with the dry ingredients, then add the eggs and finish as in the main recipe.

To make the pastry, dissolve the yeast in the warm milk with a pinch of the sugar. Cover and leave in a warm place for 10 minutes to froth.

Sift the flour into a bowl with the remaining sugar and the salt. Put the eggs in a bowl, whisk well, then make a well in the flour and pour in the eggs and the frothy yeast mixture. Mix to a soft, elastic dough. Add a little more flour if necessary, but keep the dough quite soft. Work in the softened butter until smooth, shiny and elastic. The dough will not form a ball at this stage. (If preferred, the whole process can be done easily in a large electric food mixer.)

Cover and let rise in a warm place for 2–4 hours until doubled in size (or leave overnight in the refrigerator). Knock back, then wrap and chill until firm enough to roll out – this takes about 30 minutes.

To make the custard, put the milk, cream and split vanilla pod in a saucepan and heat until almost boiling. Leave to infuse for 15 minutes. Beat the eggs, egg yolk and sugar together until pale and creamy. Remove the vanilla pod. Beat the flour into the egg mixture, then whisk in the milk and cream mixture. Set aside.

Preheat the oven to 200°C (400°F) Gas 6. Roll out the pastry and use it to line the tart tin. Pour in the custard, dot with the cherries and let rise in a warm place for 20 minutes. Bake for 15–20 minutes or until the custard is just starting to set.

Reduce the heat to 160°C (325°F) Gas 3. Brush the pastry edges with the beaten egg and bake for a further 45 minutes until golden and set. Let cool in the tin. Serve at room temperature.

Note Wash and dry the vanilla pod, then put in a sugar jar to make vanilla sugar.

Fresh dates are so sweet and sticky, they make a fantastic quick-and-easy topping for a crisp puff pastry base. The maple syrup and sugar caramelize with the butter and give the tarts a wonderful sheen. Don't serve them too hot, or you will burn your mouth.

sticky date flaky tarts with caramel oranges

1 recipe Classic Puff Pastry (page 16), Rough Puff Pastry (page 17) or Cheat's Rough Puff Pastry (page 18)

caramel oranges

4 small, juicy, thin-skinned oranges

125 g sugar

date topping

55 g unsalted butter

30 g soft light brown sugar

2 tablespoons maple syrup

12–16 fresh Medjool dates

75 g walnut pieces

a saucer or similar, 13 cm diameter (to use as a template)

a large baking sheet

serves 4

Preheat the oven to 200°C (400°F) Gas 6.

Roll out the pastry thinly on a lightly floured work surface, then cut out 4 circles 13 cm diameter, using the saucer as a guide. Put these onto a large baking sheet, prick all over, then chill or freeze for 15 minutes.

To make the caramel oranges, slice the top and bottom off each orange, then cut off the skin in a spiral, as if you were peeling an apple. Try to remove all the bitter white pith. Slice down between the membranes and flick out each segment. Catch the juice in a bowl, then squeeze the remaining juice out of the membranes.

Put the sugar and 3 tablespoons water in a heavy saucepan. Put over low heat until the liquid is clear and the sugar has completely dissolved. Increase the heat and boil until the liquid turns a dark caramel colour. Quickly remove from the heat, stand back and add another 3 tablespoons water – it will hiss and splutter.

Return the pan to the stove over low heat, and stir until all the hardened pieces of caramel have dissolved. Pour in the reserved orange juice and boil hard until very thick and syrupy. Remove from the heat and let cool completely before adding the orange segments. Chill until needed.

To make the date topping, cut the dates in half and remove the pits. Put the butter, sugar and maple syrup in a saucepan and melt over gentle heat, then add the dates and walnuts.

Spoon the mixture over the circles, leaving a small clear rim on the outside of each. Bake for 15–18 minutes until the pastry is risen and golden and the dates sizzling. Serve with the caramel oranges.

My grandmother made wonderful tartlets in bun trays and let me fill them with bright yellow shop-bought lemon curd. I don't know if she would approve of these exotic mouthfuls – they are very wicked. Remember, the more wrinkled the passionfruit, the riper the flesh inside. Why not make double the quantity of curd and pot up any you don't use?

pineapple and passionfruit curd tartlets

1 recipe Pâte Sucrée (page 14)

passionfruit curd

6 ripe, juicy passionfruit

freshly squeezed juice of
1 small lemon, strained

75 g unsalted butter, cubed

3 large eggs, beaten

225 g sugar

fruit topping

1 small fresh pineapple,
peeled, cored and sliced

4 passionfruit

a fluted biscuit cutter, 7.5 cm diameter

a 12-hole bun tray

makes 12 tartlets

Bring the pastry to room temperature before rolling out.

Cut the 6 passionfruit in half, scoop out the flesh and press through a sieve into a medium bowl to extract the juice. Add the lemon juice, butter, eggs and sugar and set over a saucepan of simmering water (or cook in a double boiler). Cook, stirring all the time, for about 20 minutes or until the curd has thickened considerably. If you are brave enough, you can cook this over direct heat, watching that it doesn't get too hot and curdle. Strain into a bowl and set aside.

Preheat the oven to 180°C (350°F) Gas 4. Roll out the pastry thinly on a lightly floured work surface and cut out 12 rounds with the biscuit cutter. Line the bun tray with the pastry, pressing it into the holes. Prick the bases and chill or freeze for 15 minutes. Bake blind for 5–6 minutes without lining with beans. Let cool.

When ready to serve, fill the tartlet cases with a spoonful of passionfruit curd, then top with sliced pineapple. Cut the 4 passionfruit in half, scoop out the flesh and spoon a little, seeds and all, over each tartlet. Serve immediately before the tartlets have a chance to become soggy.

My Scottish-Canadian cousin, Deirdre, introduced us to this pie when she lived with us in Scotland for a while, back in the 1960s. It seemed so exotic in the far north of Britain – none of us having even seen a pumpkin before, never mind cans of purée – and has remained a family favourite ever since. Butternut squash purée is an acceptable substitute if pumpkin is not available.

pumpkin pie

1 recipe American Pie Crust
(page 12)

pumpkin filling

500 ml homemade pumpkin purée
or one 475 g can

100 g light soft brown sugar

3 large eggs

200 ml evaporated milk

120 ml golden syrup

a good pinch of salt

1 teaspoon ground cinnamon

1/2 teaspoon mixed spice

1 teaspoon real vanilla essence

2 tablespoons dark rum (optional)

2 tart tins or pie plates, 22 cm diameter

makes 2 pies, 22 cm diameter

Bring the pastry to room temperature. Preheat the oven to 190°C (375°F) Gas 5.

Roll out the pastry thinly on a lightly floured work surface, then use to line the 2 tart tins or pie plates. Trim and crimp or decorate the edges as you wish. Prick the bases all over with a fork, chill or freeze for 15 minutes, then bake blind following the method given on page 22. Lower the oven to 160°C (325°F) Gas 3.

Put all the filling ingredients in a food processor and blend until smooth. Pour the mixture into the tart shells, set on a baking sheet and bake for about 1 hour or until just set. Remove from the oven and let stand for 10 minutes, then remove the tart tins and let cool for a few minutes. Serve warm or at room temperature, not chilled.

Note To make your own pumpkin purée, cut a pumpkin or butternut squash into large chunks and bake for about 1 hour at 160°C (325°F) Gas 3. Scrape the flesh from the skin and purée until smooth in a food processor.

There's nothing quite as delicious as a real custard tart. I come from a long line of bakers, and these would be one of our 'desert island' luxuries. The nutmeg is the classic flavouring here, but I infuse the milk with fresh bay leaf to add a mysterious musky scent to the custard. Fresh bay leaves should be more widely used in cooking – the flavour is like nutmeg, but 'greener' and sweeter.

little nutmeg and bay leaf custard tarts

1 recipe Pâte Sucrée (page 14)*

nutmeg and bay leaf custard

600 ml full-cream milk

3 fresh (preferably) or dried bay leaves

6 large egg yolks

75 g caster sugar

1 whole nutmeg

8 loose-based tart tins, 10 cm diameter (or use smaller but deeper tins and increase the cooking time)

2 baking sheets

a wire rack

makes about 8 tarts

*Use any leftover pastry to make a few more tarts.

Bring the pastry to room temperature. Preheat the oven to 200°C (400°F) Gas 6.

Roll out the pastry thinly on a lightly floured work surface and use to line the tart tins. Put these on a baking sheet and chill for 30 minutes.

To make the custard, put the milk and bay leaves in a saucepan and heat until lukewarm. Put the egg yolks and sugar in a bowl and beat until pale and creamy. Pour the warmed milk onto the yolks and stir well – do not whisk or you will get bubbles. Strain into a jug and pour into the tart cases. Grate fresh nutmeg liberally over the surface of the tartlets.

Preheat the other baking sheet in the oven. Put the tart tins onto the preheated sheet and bake in the oven for 10 minutes. Lower the heat to 180°C (350°F) Gas 4 and bake until set and just golden – about another 10 minutes. Don't overbake as the custard should be a bit wobbly when the tarts come out of the oven.

Remove from the tins and let cool on a wire rack. Serve at room temperature.

Note Because the tarts are not baked blind, cooking them on preheated baking sheets will help the bases to cook quickly and crisply.

This is the most beautiful and delicious tart in the world. The recipe was given to me by my sister Jacks. It tastes so delicate – and is lovely to serve at a wedding or christening.

jacks' rose petal tart

1 recipe Classic Puff Pastry (page 16) or 350 g frozen puff pastry, thawed*

plain flour, for rolling

rose-flavoured filling
150 ml Greek yoghurt
1 egg yolk
2–3 tablespoons rosewater
2 tablespoons caster sugar
300 ml double cream

crystallized rose petals
1 egg white
petals of 2–4 scented roses
caster sugar

a round or heart-shaped tart tin, 25 cm diameter

foil and baking beans

a wire rack or non-stick baking parchment

makes one 25 cm tart

To crystallize the rose petals, put the egg white in a bowl, beat until frothy, then paint onto clean, dry petals. Sprinkle with caster sugar to coat completely, then arrange on a cake rack or non-stick baking parchment and leave in a warm place to dry out and crisp – at least overnight. Cool, but do NOT put in the refrigerator. Store between layers of kitchen paper in an airtight container.

Preheat the oven to 230°C (450°F) Gas 8. Roll out the pastry as thinly as possible on a lightly floured work surface. Use to line the tart tin, pressing it into the sides and trimming to leave 5 mm hanging over the edge. Turn this inwards to make a rim. Prick the base all over with a fork, then chill or freeze for 15 minutes. Line with foil and baking beans and bake blind for 12–15 minutes. Lower the oven to 200°C (400°F) Gas 6, remove the foil and beans and return to the oven for a further 5 minutes to dry out. You may have to flatten the pastry if it puffs up.

Reduce the heat to 180°C (350°F) Gas 4. Put the yoghurt, egg yolk, rosewater and sugar in a bowl and mix well. Put the cream in a bowl and whisk until soft peaks form, then fold it into the yoghurt mixture. Spoon into the baked tart shell, level the surface and bake for about 20 minutes. It will seem almost runny, but will set as it cools. Cover and chill until firm.

Decorate with the crystallized rose petals. Serve slightly cold.

Note If using 1 recipe of homemade Classic Puff Pastry, you will have some left over to freeze for later use.

This is wickedly delicious. Use the darkest chocolate you can find and serve in thin slices. The filling is gooey and rich inside – delicious with a spoonful of sour cherry jam and another of crème fraîche. Sometimes, I spread the base of the tart with the jam before pouring in the mixture.

baked darkest chocolate mousse tart

1 recipe Pâte Sucrée (page 14)

chocolate mousse filling

400 g plain chocolate (60–70 per cent cocoa solids), broken into pieces

125 g unsalted butter, cubed

5 large eggs, separated

125 g caster sugar

150 ml double cream, at room temperature

3 tablespoons dark rum (optional)

to finish

icing sugar, to dust

cream, to serve

a deep loose-based tart tin, 25 cm diameter, 4 cm deep

foil and baking beans

serves 8

Bring the pastry to room temperature. Preheat the oven to 190°C (375°F) Gas 5.

Roll out the pastry thinly on a lightly floured work surface, then use to line the tart tin. Prick the base, then chill or freeze for 15 minutes.

Line with foil and baking beans and bake blind for 15 minutes. Remove the foil and beans, reduce the heat to 180°C (350°F) Gas 4 and return to the oven for 10–15 minutes to dry out and brown. Cool and remove from the tin, then transfer to a serving platter.

Put the chocolate and butter in a bowl and melt over a pan of simmering water. As soon as it has melted, remove the bowl from the heat and cool slightly for a minute or so.

Put the egg yolks and sugar in a bowl and whisk with an electric beater until pale and creamy. Stir the cream and the rum, if using, into the melted chocolate mixture, then quickly fold in the egg yolk mixture. Put the egg whites in a clean bowl and whisk until soft peaks form. Quickly fold into the chocolate mixture.

Pour into the tart shell and bake for 25 minutes until risen and a bit wobbly. Remove from the oven and let cool – the filling will sink and firm up as it cools. Dust with icing sugar, and serve at room temperature with cream.

This recipe comes from Carl, the chef who cooked for us in a chalet in Méribel, France, during a skiing holiday. He was a fabulous cook and a dream of a pastry chef – this is one of his specialities.

carl's chocolate pecan tart with coffee bean sauce

1 recipe Sweet Rich Shortcrust Pastry (page 10) or Pâte Sucrée (page 14)

1 egg, beaten, to glaze

cream, to serve

chocolate filling

120 g dark chocolate (at least 60 per cent cocoa solids)

50 g unsalted butter

3 large eggs, beaten

175 ml maple syrup

250 g pecan nuts

coffee bean sauce

1 vanilla pod, split

300 ml milk

1 tablespoon finely ground espresso coffee

1 tablespoon caster sugar

2 medium egg yolks

2 tablespoons cognac or Armagnac

a tart tin, 23 cm diameter

foil and baking beans

serves 6

To make the coffee bean sauce, put the vanilla pod, milk, coffee and sugar in a saucepan and heat gently. Bring almost to the boil, then set aside to infuse for 15 minutes. Remove the vanilla pod.

Put the egg yolks in a bowl, beat well, then pour in the infused milk. Mix well and return to the pan. Stir with a wooden spoon over gentle heat until the custard coats the back of the spoon. Pour into a cold bowl and stir in the cognac. Cover with clingfilm, cool and chill until needed.

Bring the pastry to room temperature. Preheat the oven to 190°C (375°F) Gas 5.

If using sweet rich shortcrust pastry, roll out on a lightly floured work surface and use to line the tart tin. Prick the base and chill or freeze for 15 minutes. Bake blind (page 22). Glaze with beaten egg and bake again for 5–10 minutes. Let cool.

If using pâte sucrée, roll out thinly on a lightly floured work surface, then use to line the tart tin. Prick the base, then chill or freeze for 15 minutes. Line with foil and baking beans and bake blind for 15 minutes. Remove the foil and beans, reduce the heat to 180°C (350°F) Gas 4 and return to the oven for 10–15 minutes to dry out and brown. Glaze with the beaten egg and bake again for 5–10 minutes. Let cool.

To make the chocolate filling, reduce the heat to 160°C (325°F) Gas 3. Break up the chocolate and put it in the top of a double boiler or a bowl set over a pan of simmering water. Add the butter and stir over gentle heat until melted.
Put the eggs and maple syrup in a bowl and beat well. Add to the the chocolate. Stir well, and keep stirring over low heat until the mixture starts to thicken. Stir in the pecan nuts and pour into the tart shell.

Bake for 35–40 minutes until just set – the filling will still be a bit wobbly. Serve warm with the sauce and cream.

My sister is responsible for this outrageous recipe. We were chatting about brownies one night and she came up with the idea of making a walnut crust for the tart instead of having the nuts in the filling. Here is the result. My niece Cassia helped stir the mixture for the tart in the photograph. Was there any ulterior motive in her kind gesture, I wonder?

double chocolate brownie tart with walnut crust

150 g digestive biscuits

150 g walnuts

125 g unsalted butter, melted

brownie filling

125 g dark plain chocolate, broken into small pieces

175 g unsalted butter

400 g caster sugar

3 large eggs, beaten

1 teaspoon real vanilla essence

150 g all-purpose flour

200 g white chocolate chips

a deep cake tin, 23 cm square

non-stick baking parchment

makes about 16 brownies

Line the base of the tin with a square of non-stick baking parchment to make removing the finished tart easier.

To make the base, crush the biscuits and walnuts in a food processor, pulsing to keep the biscuits and nuts quite coarse. Stir the biscuits into the melted butter until evenly coated. Press evenly into the base and 4 cm up the sides of the tin before it cools (a flat potato masher will help you to do this). Chill in the refrigerator for 20 minutes to set the base before filling.

Preheat the oven to 180°C (350°F) Gas 4.

To make the filling, put the chocolate in a small bowl and melt over a pan of hot water. Put the butter and sugar in a bowl, cream until light and fluffy, then beat in the eggs. Stir in the melted chocolate and vanilla. Fold in the flour, then half the chocolate chips. Spoon into the biscuit case and level the top. Sprinkle with the remaining chocolate chips.

Bake for 35 minutes or until a cocktail stick inserted in the middle reveals fudgy crumbs. Do not overcook.

Cool in the tin. When cool, turn out of the tin and cut into 16 pieces.

This soft, sticky tart packed with walnuts is superb with
the easy vanilla ice cream marbled with fudge toffee.

walnut tart
with quick fudge ice cream

1 recipe Sweet Rich Shortcrust Pastry
(page 10)

walnut filling

125 g unsalted butter, softened

125 g light soft brown sugar

3 large eggs

grated zest and juice of 1 small orange

175 g golden syrup

225 g shelled walnut pieces

a pinch of salt

quick fudge ice cream

150 g chewy toffees (such as Werther's)

100 g double cream

1 tub (600 ml) best quality vanilla
ice cream, softened

a fluted tart tin, 23 cm diameter

serves 6

Bring the pastry to room temperature. Preheat the oven to 190°C (375°F) Gas 5.

Roll out the pastry on a lightly floured work surface and use to line the tart tin. Prick the base, chill or freeze for 15 minutes, then bake blind following the method given on page 22. Cool. Lower the oven to 180°C (350°F) Gas 4.

To make the filling, put the butter and sugar in a bowl and cream until light and fluffy. Gradually beat in the eggs, one at a time. Beat the orange zest and juice into the butter and egg mixture. Heat the golden syrup in a small saucepan until runny, but not very hot. Stir into the butter mixture, then stir in the walnuts and salt.

Pour into the tart shell and bake for 45 minutes until lightly browned and risen. The tart will sink a little on cooling.

While the tart is cooling, make the ice cream. Put the toffees and double cream in a small saucepan and stir over medium heat to melt. Cool slightly and stir quickly into the ice cream so that it looks marbled. Put the ice cream back in the freezer until ready to serve.

Serve the tart at room temperature with scoops of the fudge ice cream.

A deliciously moist and almondy tart with a crust of caramelized pine nuts, perfect served with coffee or with fresh peaches and apricots.

frangipane pine nut tart

1 recipe Pâte Sucrée (page 14) or
My Just-Push-It-In Pastry (page 20)

almond filling

100 g blanched almonds

100 g caster sugar

100 g unsalted butter, softened

5 large eggs, beaten

2 tablespoons Marsala or dark rum

a pinch of salt

100 g all-purpose flour

to finish

100 g pine nuts

2 tablespoons icing sugar

a baking sheet

a loose-based tart tin, 25 cm diameter

serves 6

If using pâte sucrée, bring it to room temperature. Preheat the oven to 200°C (400°F) Gas 6, then set the baking sheet on the middle shelf.

Roll out the pastry thinly on a lightly floured work surface, use to line the tart tin and prick the base all over. Alternatively, line the tin with my just-push-it-in pastry rounds. Chill or freeze for 15 minutes.

To make the almond filling, put the almonds and sugar in a food processor and grind until the almonds are as fine as possible. Add the butter and blend until creamy. Gradually blend in the beaten eggs, then add the Marsala and the pinch of salt. Finally, add the flour, blending quickly until just mixed.

Spread the filling over the base of the tart, then sprinkle with the pine nuts. Don't worry if there seems to be too little filling – it will rise.

Bake on the preheated baking sheet for about 10 minutes, until the pastry begins to brown at the edges, then lower the heat to 180°C (350°F) Gas 4 and bake for a further 20 minutes until puffed, brown and set.

Remove the tart from the oven and turn up the heat to 230°C (450°F) Gas 8. Sift the icing sugar over the top in a thin and even layer. Return to the oven for 5 minutes or less, until the sugar melts and caramelizes. (Alternatively, put under a preheated grill, protecting the pastry edges with foil, for a couple of minutes until the sugar caramelizes.) Serve warm.

Note Because the tart is not baked blind, cooking it on a preheated baking sheet will help to make the base cook quickly and crisply.

index